CHURCHES
OF ENGLAND

By Colin Pitt

ISBN 978-1-7398450-8-7

CP PRESS

Published August 2022

INTRODUCTION

Churches of England looks at churches by famous architects such as George Edmund Street, Basil Champneys, John Dando Sedding, Charles Harrison Townsend, Frederick Gibberd, Richard Norman Shaw, Giles Gilbert Scott, Richard Gilbert Scott, Harry Stuart Goodhart-Rendell, Nugent Cachemaille-Day and Edwin Lutyens.

CONTENTS

The Abbey church is Grade II listed and the architect was Francis Pollen.

Construction of Our Lady Help of Christians, a Roman Catholic Abbey church, began in 1965 and was completed in 1975.

All Saints, Ealing Common was designed 1903-1905 by William Alfred Pite who was the brother of Professor Beresford Pite, architect of Christ Church, Brixton.

All Saints, Ealing Common is the Spencer Perceval Memorial Church built when his youngest daughter bequethed money in her will to erect a church in his memory. Spencer Perceval was Prime Minister of Britain from 1809 to 1812 until his death in 1812. He was assassinated in the House of Commons by John Bellingham.

All Saints Church, Boyne Hill, Maidenhead, Berkshire is a Grade I listed church. It was completed in 1857 and is one of the finest examples of the early work of George Edmund Street.

George Edmund Street, popularised the Victorian Gothic style.

All Saints, Ennismore Gardens was built 1846 - 1849 by L. Vulliamy but the front was built in 1892 by C. H. Townsend.

All Saints, is decorated in Arts and Crafts Sgrafitto by Heywood Sumner. It is now the Dormation of the Mother of God and All Saints of the Russian Orthodox Church.

The contract for All Saints, Margaret Street was signed on 1st September 1850 and went to John Kelk a West End builder based in Margaret Street.

All Saints Day 1852 had been the date aimed at for consecration but the church stayed shut for several years after this with differences over how to finish the interior being the main reason for delays. The church was finally consecrated in May 1859 with estimated expenditure in the region of £70,000 and The Prince Consort was among early visitors to All Saints.

The church's plan consisted of a three-bay nave that was about double the width of the flanking aisles, and a two-bay chancel. The westernmost bay of the nave on the South side supports the tower, triplets of windows over the arches alternate with wider blanks over the piers.

The colour and patterns visible in All Saints date from the original finishes of 1852, the decoration of the later 1850's, Butterfield's additions and alterations between the 1870's and 1890's, Comper's alterations after 1909 and restoration by Colin Kerr since 2007.

All Saints was built 1849 - 1859 to the designs of architect William Butterfield.

William Butterfield was also the architect of St. Augustine, Queens Gate.

The Church of Holy Redeemer at 24 Exmouth Market, Angel was built in 1887 by J. D. Sedding.

In giant gilt letters 'Christo Liberator" stands above the entrance.

The Friary Church of St. Francis and St. Anthony is a Roman Catholic church in Crawley.

The Friary Church was listed Grade II on 25 October 2007 and is one of the best works by H. S. Goodhart-Rendel.

London's Arts and Crafts church by John Dando Sedding, built 1888 - 1890.

The stained glass of the east windows was made by Morris and Company to the designs of Burne-Jones.

Holy Trinity, Sloane Street: the pulpit.

Inside Holy Trinity there is an excellent display of furnishings and decoration by some of the best artists with Arts & Crafts connections.

The chancel gates in virtuoso wrought iron are Sedding's most dazzling work.

The bronze angel lecturn is by Henry Hugh Armstead, Hamo Thorneycroft carved the stone corbels and Onslow Ford designed the font.

St. Augustine Roman Catholic Church was designed by Desmond Williams Associates.

The building, listed Grade II, is on an east-west axis with seating either side of a central aisle and an altar occupying the west end.

St Augustine's was built 1870 - 1877 by John Pearson.

St. Augustine's is sometimes called the Cathedral of North London on account of its grandeur. The tower is seventy-seven metres high.

Pearson was also the architect for Truro Cathedral and St. Margaret's, Westminster.

Pearson was a Gothic Revival architect.

St. Barnabas, Ealing was built in 1916 by architect Ernest Shearman.

Ernest Shearman designed six London churches between 1910 and 1936. St. Matthew, Wimbledon (destroyed), St. Silas, Kentish Town (1913), St. Barnabas, Ealing (1916), St. Gabriel, Acton (1931), St. Barnabas, Temple Fortune (1934) and St. Francis of Assisi, Osterley (1935).

All except one of Ernest Shearman's churches show a fascination with rose windows.

St. Barnabas is very atmospheric inside.

The main body of the Church of St. Francis of Assisi, Pottery Lane, was built by Jackson and Shaw in 1859-1860 to the designs of Henry Clutton. The building work was supervised by John Francis Bentley and the church opened on 2nd February 1860.

Bentley designed additions including the presbytery and school which were completed by 1863. The school and presbytery are in the same thirteenth-century French Gothic style as the church.

St. George, Hanover Square was built 1721 - 1724 by John James.

The portico is Corinthian and the north and south elevations each have five bays. Inside are galleries on piers, topped with Corinthian columns supporting the vaulted ceiling.

St Ignatius occupies a corner site with frontages on Stamford Hill and St. Ann's Road. The architects were Benedict and J. H. Beart Foss.

St. Ignatius is ministered by the Society of Jesus who founded it on 1894. The Jesuits decided to dedicate the church to their order's founder, St. Ignatius of Loyola.

The principal dimensions of St. Ignatius Church are a Nave of 105 feet by 32 feet and 53 feet high, a Sanctuary of 37 feet by 32 feet and Towers of 14 feet 9 inches by 14 feet 9 inches and 119 feet high to the ridge of the roof.

The exterior of St. Ignatius Church is faced with two-inch Belgian bricks with Kentish Rag and reconstructed-stone dressings. Green Westmoreland slates cover the roof. Glazing and headed Glass Work were by William Morris & Co. Ltd.

St. James, Piccadilly was built 1676 - 1684 by Christopher Wren but Albert Richardson added the copper spire. Wren thought a congregation of two thousand people could be accomodated.

The virtuoso alterpiece carvings are by Grinling Gibbons.

St. John was built 1744 - 1747. The interior was altered in 1872 by S. P. Cockerell and Ionic columns support arches which cut into the tunnel vault.

Those buried here include George du Maurier, John Constable and Richard Norman Shaw.

St. John, Waterloo Road, Waterloo was built 1822 - 1824 by F. O. Bedford.

It is one of the many 'Waterloo churches' built by the Church Commissioners.

The Church of St. John the Evangelist is a Grade II listed church. It was consecrated in 1874 on land bought from the Box Moor Trust.

Richard Norman Shaw was the architect and it was designed in the Gothic Revival style.

St. John's Wood Chapel was built in 1813 by Thomas Hardwick.

Inside Tuscan columns support glazed galleries.

The original site of the Royal College of St. Katherine had been next to the Tower of London.

In 1825 the hospital was rebuilt in Regent's Park. It was designed by Ambrose Poynter.

St Luke's Church was built between 1867 and 1869 by Basil Champneys, using compensation money provided by the railway company for the demolition of St. Luke's Church, Euston Road.

St Luke's is a Grade II* listed building.

St. Martin-in-the-fields was built 1721 - 1726 by James Gibbs. There was a redevelopment by Eric Parry Associates (2006 - 2008) and you now see a freestanding glass entrance kiosk in the passage north of the church.

To the east end there is a large Venetian window with newly created glass by Shirazeh Housiary. The interior has galleries on three sides with a vault over the nave on Corinthian columns.

This Arts and Crafts church is by C. Harrison Townsend and the interior consists of nave and transepts but no aisles. The rood is panelled in wood and the roof has ribs of aluminium leaf, decorated with reliefs of giant rose trees, each resting on a panel of lilies.

Font, pulpit and lectern are Art Nouveau.

St. Mary Woolnoth was built 1716 - 1727 by Nicholas Hawksmoor and occupies a site on Lombard Street and King William Street. The 'Tower' is so broad that it occupies almost the full width of the West front

The interior is square with an inner square defined by twelve Corinthian columns bunched into the corners. There were alterations to the interior in 1875 - 1876 by Butterfield resulting in galleries previously occupying the north and south sides being dismantled.

In choosing a parishoner as architect, the Vestry selected Thomas Hardwick of Berners Street. With St. John's Wood Chapel well advanced Hardwick was appointed to design the New Road chapel in April 1813. Thomas Hardwick's design went out to tender in June 1813 and the lowest bidder was Richard Wade. By June 1814 the Vestry decided Hardwick should aggrandize the chapel into a church. The final cost in 1817 was estimated at around £62,000. Sculptor Henry Westmacott was commissioned to model the capitals for the columns and pilasters. Consecration, originally scheduled for 31 December, took place on 4 February 1817. The public face of St. Mary towards Marylebone Road with an approach from the north was acquired when Nash's York Gate was laid out.

Above the church and garden can be seen from the south-east.

The interior originally had two levels of galleries on three sides supported by slender iron columns. The upper galleries on the north and south sides were removed in the late nineteenth century by Thomas Harris.

Superb interior of St. Mary, Marylebone Road.

St. Mary-le-Strand was built 1714 - 1717 by James Gibbs. Gibbs was Hawksmoor's contemporary. The church is now stranded on a large traffic island. The inside has neither aisles nor galleries but is a simple box with a coffered segmental vault.

At 68 metres, St. Mary-le-Bow is second only to St. Bride in height.

St. Mary-le-Bow was built 1670 - 1683 by Christopher Wren.

St. Mary's symmetrical west front has a centre tower of London stock brick.

The church was built 1824 - 1827 by W. and H. W. Inwood.

St. Mary, Wyndham Place, was built in 1823 by Robert Smirke.

Smirke's use of the Greek Revival Style is seen with the gallery and the doric columns supporting the curved coffered ceiling.

St. Michael and All Angels was built 1879 - 1880 by Richard Norman Shaw as was the Tabard Inn and Stores just opposite.

The four-bay nave is in red brick with small perpendicular and rectagonal stone windows.

The tiled roof has a white timber railing to the eaves.

Maurice Adams added the Parish Hall and north aisle in 1887.

St. Nicholas Burnage, Manchester was built in 1932 and is one of Cachemaille-Day's most important pre-war churches. It is listed Grade II*.

Cachemaille-Day also built St. Savior in Eltham in 1933 and St. Michael & All Angels in Northenden, Greater Manchester in 1937.

St. Paul, Covent Garden was built 1631 - 1638 by Inigo Jones.

The main door to the church is through Inigo Place off Bedford Street. This is the other side of the church.

In 1795 a fire destroyed the interior and the restoration by Thomas Hardwick failed to replace the side galleries.

The Earl of Bedford instructed Inigo Jones saying he only wanted a church like a barn. Inigo Jones said that he would build the 'handsomest barn in England.' The church is also known as the actor's church.

St. Paul is a Grade II listed Anglican church built in 1843 by Thomas Cundy.

The building was consecrated in 1843 and the chancel with its rood screen and striking reredos was added in 1892 by G. F. Bodley.

The west front of St. Peter's Church, Ealing.

St. Peter's church was built between 1892 and 1893 and the new building was designed by John Dando Sedding architect of Holy Trinity, Sloane Street but following Sedding's death was built under the direction of designer and architect Henry Wilson.

Wilson's hand can be seen in the plates on the West porch interior doors. The font was designed by Leonard Shuffrey.

The Lady Chapel at St. Peter's Ealing was restored in 2022 and the paintings in it are by Henry Brewer.

The Grade II* listed building is noted for its combination of Arts & Crafts and late-Victorian Gothic.

The Parish Church of St. Peter, Great Berkhamsted is a Grade II* listed church in Berkhamsted, Hertfordshire.

In 1870-1871 another restoration programme was carried out by the Gothic Revival architect William Butterfield.

The Oxford Chapel, known since 1832 as St. Peter's Vere Street, was built 1721 - 1724 for the inhabitants of houses around Cavendish Square. The building is no longer a chapel but the home of the London Institute for Contemporary Christianity. It is the sole survivor in its original form of Marylebone's 18th - century proprietary chapels.

The Oxford Chapel was paid for by Lord Harley and designed by James Gibbs. Gibbs was also responsible for St. Mary le Strand (1714 - 1717) and Gibbs had also extended the Harley's house at Wimpole, Cambridgeshire.

The chapel is essentially a rectangular grey-brick box that incorporates a western ante-chapel, with galleries on three sides reached by stairs either side of the ante-chapel. Arcades of giant Corinthian columns on high pedestals carry the galleries. The ceiling of the main vault has Artari and Bagutti's Italian rococo plasterwork. It was here that in 1734 that the Earl of Oxford's daughter, Lady Margeret Harley, married the 2nd Duke of Portland. In 1817 the Crown bought the Oxford Chapel and other proprietary chapels in the area from the 4th Duke of Portland.

In 1982 - 1983 the church was adapted for the London Institute for Contemporary Christianity. Timber and glass partitions were inserted under the galleries to make offices and reading rooms. The galleries on the north side were converted into a library.

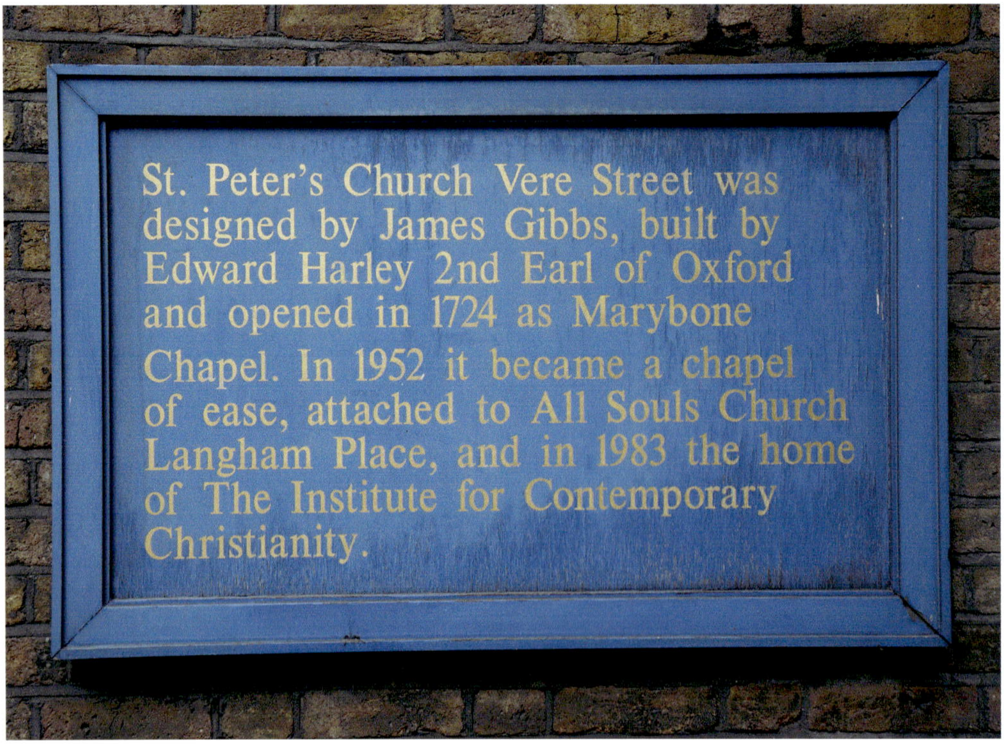

Theologian F. D. Maurice succeeded the Rev. Edward Scobell and preached here from 1860 until 1869.

St. Peters Vere Street, has a stained glass window designed by Edward Burne-Jones.

St. Peters Vere Street became a daughter church of All Souls, Langham Place, for which it stood in during post-war rebuilding there.

St. Peters Italian Catholic Church is a basilica-style church that was consecrated 16 April 1863 and built by the architect Sir John Miller-Bryson. The frontal section of the church consists of a loggia and portico with twin arches, above which are three alcoves.

St. Peters Italian Catholic Church is modelled on the Basilica San Crisogono in Rome.

The church was built at the request of Saint Vincent Pallotti and remains under the control of the Pallotine order which he founded.

The church was intended for the growing number of Italian immigrants in London in the mid 19th century.

St. Patrick's was built 1891 - 1893 by Kelly and Birchall.

St Patrick's is one of several churches in Soho to have served various generations of settlers.

St. Saviour church, Eltham is one of the earliest Modern Movement buildings dating from 1932-1933.

The architects were Welch, Lander and Nugent Cachemaille-Day and inside it has blue slit windows above the altar.

The church has one of the finest steeples in England. Wailes contributed the west windows and Blomfield the reredos.

The interior of St. Wulfram's is a single rectangle, its atmosphere dominated by George Gilbert Scott's Victorian roofs and rood screen.

Sheffield's Trinity United Reformed Church was designed by J. Mansell Jenkinson and Son.

The church was built 1970-1971 and the gold cross above the pulpit is by the Sheffield designer David Mellor.

There are two churches dominating Central Square's hilltop and both are the work of architect Sir Edwin Lutyens. They are this one - The Free Church and St. Jude's.

The Free Church has a central dome while the other church in Central Square - St. Jude's - has a spire.

The Church of the Immaculate Conception, Farm Street, was built 1844-1849 by J. J. Scoles. The high altar was by Augustus Welby Pugin.

There are entrances from both Farm Street and Mount Street Gardens to the church. The nave and aisles are of eight bays.

Westminster Cathedral, Archbishop's House and Clergy House were built 1895 - 1903 by John Francis Bentley.

John Francis Bentley was asked by Cardinal Vaughan to build Westminster Cathedral in Byzantine style possibly to avoid stylistic competition with Westminster Abbey.

The church has a great nave roofed with three shallow concrete coppered domes. The nave is flanked with narrow aisles with galleries above.

The side chapels are finished with much mosaic above the marble.

The Cathedral's architects were members of the Cardiff-based Percy Thomas Partnership.

The design team were Frederick Jennett, Ronald Weeks and Antoni Perembo. There is a spacious hexagonal sanctuary and no one is more than 50 feet from the High Altar.

Quinlan Terry was the architect and the north walls are built of Kentish ragstone divided by Doric Pilasters in Portland stone.

Inside the cathedral light from leaded windows floods in.

Classical interior of the cathedral at Brentwood. Behind the Bishop's chair the Blessed Sacrement Chapel was created.

In the centre is a giant portico that bulges out in a semi-circle.

The money for the cathedral was given anonymously. Architect Quinlan Terry was inspired by the early Italian Renaissance.

The huge vaulted, complex interior is opulently decorated.

The Newcastle firm of A. M. Dunn and E. J. Hansom won the design competition. A local firm, Rattee and Kett were appointed builders. The sanctuary was re-ordered in 1973 by Gerard Goalen, the architect of the church of Our Lady of Fatima at Harlow.

Designed by another member of the Scott dynasty - Richard Gilbert Scott - who joined his father Sir Giles Gilbert Scott as a partner in 1953.

The design demanded new materials and state-of-the-art technology as well as a new approach to the art of stained glass.

From a central space you can look across the congregation to glowing bands of blue and white glass.

Stained glass windows are the work of John Chrestien.

Our Lady of the Rosary has been a Grade II Listed Building since 25th September 1998.

The church and presbytery were built 1959-1962, designed by H. S. Goodhart-Rendel.

Messrs Myers and Wilson were appointed builders and work began on 8 September 1840 on Pugin's second design.

On the night of 15 - 16 April 1941 the timber roof was fired by an incendiary bomb. The whole Cathedral was gutted.

In August 1953 work commenced under the architect Romilly B. Craze and the builders were Higgs & Hill. The formal reopening took place on 4 July 1958.

The Cathedral was changed in several ways from that of Pugin's. Pugin's slender nave piers were replaced with piers of more substantial profile. Nave walls were heightened. Aisles were given skeleton vaulting. The roods of both aisles are octopartite, with flying ribs and panels designed by Robert Hendra and Geoffrey Harper.

In 1960 the competition for the most important Catholic commission was announced by Archbishop Heenan. The winner from nearly 300 entries was Frederick Gibberd who had designed Harlow New Town and the Somerford Grove Estate in Hackney.

Thirteen chapels leading off the great central space show works of art commissioned after the church's completion.

Deep colours are infused into the Cathedral from the glass in the corona above and from great slits of glass between the walls of concrete at the sides.

The exterior buttresses give the Cathedral something of the appearance of a great tent.

Liverpool Cathedral is based on a design by Giles Gilbert Scott and is the eighth largest church in the world. Designed in the Gothic Revival style it is a Grade I listed building.

Liverpool Cathedral is the Cathedral of the Anglican Diocese of Liverpool and is also known as the Cathedral Church of the Risen Christ.

The church of St. Mary, a chapel of ease to Dorking parish church has a barrel-vaulted ceiling and is Grade II* listed. It was designed by architect Sir Edwin Lutyens in 1903.